The Dare to Blossom Rediscovery Cards Companion Guide

Mary Lunnen

Contents

Dedication and Acknowledgements 4

Foreword 6

The Source 9

Suggestions on how to use this book 14

    Spreads 15

    Other stories 17

The Words.. 21

References and Resources 122

Dedication

This book is dedicated to everyone who has helped me along the way to this point, and those who read this and who I will meet in the future.

Thank you

Acknowledgements

The quotes in the 'Experiences' section for each word are reprinted here with kind permission of friends on the dedicated Facebook group, along with some of my own reflections.

All the definitions, and the notes on the origins of words are referenced in the Cambridge Dictionary online, accessed in 2016. http://dictionary.cambridge.org.

Front and back cover: my own photograph and design.

If you have bought the book without the Dare to Blossom Rediscovery Cards, and would like to obtain a pack – please visit www.daretoblossom.co.uk, where you can buy them direct from me.

Finally, it is such a joy to be able to include the Foreword from Nick Williams. He has been an inspiration to me ever since I read his book *The Work We Were Born to Do,* many years ago now.

Foreword

I recently went on a song writing course for the first time at the grand age of 58, specifically aimed to help you write great pop songs.

I don't play a musical instrument and I have not written a song. It wasn't an understatement to say that I put myself way outside my comfort zone.

Even though I have had 14 books published, given talks around the world to hundreds of people and done hundreds of media interviews, I felt I was an absolute beginner, exposed and empty handed and very vulnerable.

But something in my soul had drawn me there. I know the power that great songs and great music have had on me since I was a child, and first hearing the Beatles and the Who on the radio growing up in Hornchurch in Essex.

I learned so much about the structure of songs, something about melody and we listened to successful songs to see how and why they worked so well.

And I have allowed myself to dream that maybe, just maybe, I could blossom in to being a song writer. I am allowing myself to dream that I could write a song that moves other people like certain songs have moved me.

Maybe there is a song writer innately in me that wants to blossom. I will discover. One of the most significant aspects of the song writing course was the enthusiasm and encouragement of our tutor, who wanted us all to blossom in to the best song writers we could be. That was precious.

We all have so much that lies innate within us, and it would seem that it should be easy to let it out. Sometimes it is, and other times we find ourselves battling against our own internal resistance.

We find it hard to give ourselves the permission to be an "adult beginner." We doubt ourselves and tell ourselves that no-one is interested in our creative expression.

I love what Mary has created here. I love the tenderness, validation and authentic sense of possibility that she has infused this book and cards with.

We all need an encourager, a cheerleader who wants us to blossom and who celebrates our every step along the way.

Mary wants to be that person for you. She wants you to be surprised and delighted by the creativity in the world right now and surprised and delighted with your own creative expression.

She wants to help you tend and cultivate your own inner creative garden so you can blossom in to what you were created to become.

Thank you Mary for cheering us all on.

Nick Williams, best-selling author of fourteen books including *The Work We Were Born To Do*

www.iamnickwilliams.com

The Source

People ask me 'What was the source of your words?'
Here are the words I wrote from my heart one day in
response.

Walking on the cliffs at Crugmeer to rediscover the
Source - of the words, of everything. I rediscovered the
child - at first growing up in the New Forest amongst the
majestic trees and open heaths. The child who heard
the voice say: You are safe my child. In the dark of night,
then forgot that voice, that message, that absolute
certainty and truth - for many, many years.

The child who loved the mossy banks of the little wood
opposite the Cornish farm cottage; who cupped the day
old chicks in her hands. The child who started to
disconnect at her first school where she was punished
with a ruler across her outstretched palm, in front of the
whole school, for a 'crime' she did not commit.

The child who safely walked these paths, these same
cliff paths, here around Trevone. Who adored watching
the same sea with all its moods from serene to stormy.
Who admired the delicate but tough plants - thrift,
spring squill, samphire - flowering on the cliffs, amongst
the rocks, despite the salt spray and tearing winds. The
child who looked out at the blue horizon towards
Ireland and America beyond, dreaming.

The little girl who lay on her back on the fragrant, springy wild thyme on the hill on Dartmoor, watching the clouds pass by, wondering what was up there. The child who knew she was part of All, all of this - the huge magnificent wild and gentleness of nature.

Losing the connection has been part of my journey, as it is for many others. Coming back to nature and the sea has always been my solace and my saviour. My true self has always known, always been 'plugged in' to the Source energy (whatever name you may use for that). Always been aware that I am part of the All, and the All is within me.

That there is nothing wrong, nothing to be fixed, nowhere to go. I am already here, already in that place called 'there'. I already have the wisdom within. All I needed was a guide to help me realise this, to find my way home to myself. The home that was always there with me, in my heart.

I began writing this piece hoping to answer the question people ask: Where did the words come from? What was the source? I am not sure if I can answer - I know the idea came to me and I designed them very quickly using an on-line print programme. The best answer I can give is the one many writers and creators give: that the idea was already there, already formed, just waiting for me to pluck it out of the field of possibility and bring it into the physical world. And, having done that, to send the idea, the words, out there for people to use as they wish.

The ways people find are constantly surprising and delighting me. The words are an entity with a life of their own. Each pack takes on a particular meaning to the person handling and enjoying them - as some have eloquently expressed in the next chapter - as a companion, an ally, a friend.

The purpose of this book is not to 'tell' you how to use the cards, to lay down any rules or 'shoulds' or 'oughts'. It is simply to share some experiences - mine and those of others - as an additional companion along the way for you.

The cards were developed in late 2011, initially to be used in workshops I was planning for 2012 on the theme 'Seeing You, Being You'. Like many people, I have used various card packs for years: the original little Angel cards; others from well-known spiritual writers; goddess cards; Hawaiian oracle cards; Medicine cards. Each of my packs is loved and well-used. Each has a character of its own and a place in my life.

Yet, still, I was inspired to create an addition to this wide selection. And I really have no clear memory of the process: I know I wrote down several lists of words as I still have a notebook containing those lists. Once I put those into the programme I chose a colour intuitively for the background of each word. The standard back of each card is my personal emblem using my own photograph of the cerise passionflower that grows in my conservatory. This flower exemplifies Dare to Blossom so perfectly with its tight buds that eventually break and bloom into glorious blossoms.

('Dare to Blossom' was inspired by the Anais Nin quote: ...and then the day came when the risk to remain tight in a bud was more painful than the risk it took to blossom.")

At first, the cards were not for sale, I simply used them as an inspirational resource, a prompt. Quite soon people started asking me to buy a pack for themselves. As they went out around the world, people began sending me back the stories of how they use them, often in ways I would not have thought of: face up; face down; with children at the beginning or end of a day; with the whole family; at the end of healing sessions.

I use them every day for myself, and with people in coaching sessions on the phone, via Skype, or in person. Some of the accounts included here are written by those people: describing the process of being open to exploring their own inner wisdom, prompted by a word or a colour - or even part of a word in some cases. Each person's experience, and each session with the same person, is totally different.

My role in a coaching session is in creating a quiet, safe space where you can be heard, hear your own voice, and be witnessed. My wish is that by using the cards you will create this place for yourself, and that maybe this book will be a companion to assist you in doing that in more depth.

Suggestions on how to use this book

My first suggestion is that if you have your own pack of cards – just get them out and shuffle them, maybe spread them out and look at the words. Absorb the colours. Start using them. Rely on your own intuition. Set the intention to rediscover your own inner wisdom.

If you do not have the cards, this book itself can be used in the same way. Flick through the pages, or open the book at random and see what the word on that page prompts for you. Sometimes I use books like this upside down when doing this to get around that tendency for them to open on the same page.

Either way, you may like to have your journal to hand to jot down any thoughts. Often that may be "Oh, I don't like this word!" If that happens to you there is always the option of putting the card back, or closing the book, and choosing again.

If you and I were on a Skype call together, or even better in a room around a table – I would gently suggest you sit with the word, and answer some of the questions with the first thoughts that come into you mind. Or, put it to one side and get on with your day, seeing what insights arise later.

Another option is to shuffle again and draw another

word, often called a 'clarifying card'. If you do this you may find that this word has a message for you, and then when you look at it with the first one there is an additional revelation for you.

There will be some examples later in this chapter to show you how all this may work, as well as the short quotes from my own experiences and those that others have kindly allowed me to share with you.

Spreads

Many types of cards suggest that you use spreads in different formats. What I have found to work most easily is simply drawing cards in succession, considering each and then looking at them together and seeing what wider picture is presented for you. Some people I have worked with have found great pleasure, and treasure, in playing with the order; making sentences; even stories – out of their words and the colours too.

One spread that has worked well for me is a simple 'Past, Present, Future' one – with an additional card underneath which they all lead to – giving you additional guidance.

You will find your own favourite ways of using these cards. People have shared some examples here.

With children

This story was sent to me by a friend in the USA, with the children, she spreads the cards out with the words visible so they can make a deliberate choice:

"I have used the Rediscovery Cards with my grandchildren in the following ways.   They were visiting and attending, day camp and each morning I had them choose a card that spoke of their intention for the day. They really enjoyed this and it opened discussion each day as we drove to the camp. Then at pick up time it also supported more conversation about their intention as they explored their day.   It fostered both communication and mindfulness of their day hopefully inviting these skills into their daily life.

"In preparation for their return home with their mother and for their starting of school in a couple of weeks I asked them, to choose a card reflecting on their intention for the new school year. Their mother and both my husband and I also chose cards. We then took turns talking about the cards we chose. Again this exercise supported communication and mindfulness.

"Another way I use the Rediscovery Cards is with my daily prayers and meditation.   I have an altar that I daily visit and say prayers.   I will choose one and sometimes two Rediscovery Cards to be part of my journey for that day.   I meditate on the chosen card and am always impressed that it seems to be a needed message for that time to guide me on my path."

Another story, from a member of my family:

"Mary gave me a lovely pack of Dare to Blossom cards for Christmas (or was it my birthday?). While I was using them myself, my two daughters - then 8 and 5 years old - wanted to join in. For the 5-year-old, this was a great way to practice her reading and word recognition and meanings of words, as well as colours. With my 8-year-old, we had some great discussions about what the words meant and also used them for spelling practice, picking five words a day for her to learn to spell. Later on, we also used them for her to be able to choose a card that described how she felt - or more positively (usually when things weren't going so well!) - how she would like to feel. The girls also made up card games to play with each other, which usually involved grouping them into colours.

Other stories

I often give talks to groups. However short the time available, I always wish to give those present a chance to try out the power of the cards for themselves.

Two days after one such talk at a meeting, I received this message:

"Hi Mary, just thought I would thank you for the gift you gave me on the Tuesday evening workshop. The word I picked from your cards is potentially the key to getting over a life threatening illness I am fighting at the moment... It didn't mean that much on the evening but it became the obvious behaviour that I hope will be the key to better health for me in the future... Thanks again."

Quite some time later I received this from the same person:

"It's so strange because the colour orange of the card stayed with me, causing me to buy an orange scarf to brighten up an outfit for my recent travels to a detox retreat in Thailand... which led on to me painting my nails orange which made me feel so good and they looked amazing. I will know if my treatment worked in a few weeks so I will let you know if the forgiveness exercise added to the success of the trial medication I was taking. I, like you, do not believe in coincidence and it was certainly no coincidence that I attended your workshop and I chose that word and colour I am sure."

And, a little later:

"The treatment worked and I am still painting my nails orange. Orange for me is the colour of a sunset in my life, as I am in the early sunset of my life right now. A peaceful healing colour bringing a day to close for a brighter tomorrow."

This is a testimonial following an on-line video call, where I shuffled and drew cards rather than the person having their own.

"Mary has a beautiful soft and gentle energy that easily guided me to some powerful insights in a short period of time. Without giving advice or solutions I felt so held and led in the answers I was looking for & her Dare to Blossom cards were such a great additional tool! They may seem simple at first glance yet hold so much depth and insight. It was an added layer to our conversation that I really deeply appreciated."

Coaches and therapists

Many people who have bought the cards use them with their own clients. At the end of a healing session for example, or even in conjunction with other types of card reading.

Two coaching colleagues provided these words:

"Mary's Rediscovery Pack provides simple prompts for self-inquiry or exploration with a group. Try them."
Ray Charlton, Alchemy of Coaching.

"Choosing a card encourages time to pause and reflect. And the words selected are always surprisingly relevant." Jackie Fletcher, Transitions Life Coaching.

This was an unsolicited testimonial received from the person who was my own first life coach, to whom I owe all this:

"This is not a polite little thank you note for your rediscovery cards, but a full-on raving fan letter! It has been such a positive experience using them in my journaling - affirming, insightful and fruitful. They are a terrific resource. Aside from the benefit of using them they are delightful in their own right - beautifully produced and lovely to handle. I've taken to carrying them around in my bag in case I have a spare few minutes to sit and draw one out to reflect on or write about.

As someone with a particular faith I have found that they dovetail very well my other practices of prayer and contemplation, and that often my writing blends these elements together to nourish and sustain my spirituality.

So a big thank you for devising and creating them, and I hope they continue to be a blessing to all those who have acquired and use them."

Thank you so much to the people quoted here.

The Words

Abundance

Colour: Turquoise blue

Definition: the situation in which there is more than enough of something. Plentifulness of the good things of life; prosperity.

Origin: Middle English: from Latin abundantia, from abundant- 'overflowing', from the verb abundare.

Prompts for you:

What is your first response to the word?

To the colour?

What else is there?

What else is there?

What are your experiences of Abundance?

How would you define what Abundance means to you?

Do you feel in your heart that you truly deserve Abundance?

Experiences:

"Good word, good colour, good intention. I welcome the abundance of the universe to enter my life and to help me spread blessings of abundance to others."

"Abundance this morning to me speaks of how much I have to be grateful for. And exciting times that are unfolding in front of me... without conscious effort from me merely need for a willingness to be open to that which is coming my way."

"Abundance from the turquoise universe is soooo different from how we think of things like money. It flows at us from all directions in many forms with little effort and great joy."

Acceptance

Colour: soft purple/lavender

Definition: The act of taking or receiving something offered. The action of consenting to receive or undertake something offered.

Prompts for you:

What is your first response to the word?

To the colour?

What else is there?

What else is there?

What are your experiences of Acceptance?

How would you define what Acceptance means to you?

Is there anything you accept too easily? Or that you have a barrier to accepting?

Experiences:

"Much needed for my situation at work, And, at home, it seems now."

"Acceptance of oneself and acceptance that everything happens for a reason."

"Key to life."

"Accepting when I need a rest before I can support other people is essential."

"For me this is not about giving in or being passive, rather it is more active, more about the practical. 'This has happened, what is a good way to go forward?'"

Action

Colour: dark blue

Definition: The fact or process of doing something, typically to achieve an aim.

Prompts for you:

What is your first response to the word?

To the colour?

What else is there?

And, what else is there?

What are your experiences of Action?

How would you define what Action means to you?

Does the thought of taking action excite you? Scare you? Why?

Experiences:

"Time for me to spring out of bed and leap into action."

"I have plenty to do for my business!"

"This is perfect for my week as we gear up for a big event this weekend for my husband's business. The card is reminding me of the need of calm, focused actions towards the goal of being ready; even while the excitement of everything that is happening with his business is swirling around us."

"Perfect word for me today. After 2 week's delay on my house renovations, I finally have action!"

"This is definitely the word for me today, although personally as well as work wise. My word today is fun! So after a day of action and getting things done I am off out this evening with some friends for a meal and fun."

"A commanding word. I automatically filled in an exclamation point at the end."

"True blue, speaks to me of obligations."

Adventure

Colour: bright pink

Definition: An unusual and exciting or daring experience.

Prompts for you:

What is your first response to the word?

To the colour?

What else is there?

And, what else is there?

What are your experiences of Adventure?

How would you define what Adventure means to you?

Experiences:

"A beautiful soft red denoting a gentle approach to one's sense of adventure."

"Suggests I need to pack up my car and take myself and my products to an event at an old people's home today and offer them facials."

"I am happy to adventure into some long awaited papers and admin soon! Later got my date to go to 5 Rhythms, it's been a while!"

"I spent much of yesterday digging into a box of diaries and letters of distant adventures - which in turn has energised me today."

"A new relationship began last night that I would call an adventure. And, I always had good times when I wore red....sounds like a sign."

"Red to me is brave courage and fire. Go out, be brave, be courageous, feel the fire in your belly and have that adventure. Red is strong so BE strong, go do it!"

Angels

Colour: turquoise/aqua blue

Definition: An attendant spirit, especially a benevolent one.

Origin: Old English engels, ultimately via ecclesiastical Latin from Greek angelos 'messenger'; superseded in Middle English by forms from Old French angele.

Prompts for you:

What is your first response to the word?

To the colour?

What else is there?

And, what else is there?

What are your experiences of Angels?

How would you define what Angels mean to you?

Experiences:

"Interesting, I had a spirit animal (a spider) appear in my sleep. Spiders spook me out, so I'm glad it wasn't a real one as it crawled under my pillow."

"Angels on turquoise.. turquoise reminds me of a beautiful summers sky and the ocean, reminding us Angels are around us always in so many places, helping, guiding, protecting but we all have to remember they can't help unless we ask them to as they're not allowed to interfere with our own free will. Love Angels so much."

"Oh Angels are always dear to me and I love that they are so uplifting, the colour is deeply soothing and healing."

"A couple of days ago I went into my home office and found a feather under my chair where I know there was not one the night before. I have a small vase of feathers that I believe me to me by the way of angels. Makes me feel protected."

"My mother loved turquoise & I have a few of her favourite pieces. she passed away almost 23 years ago. So - for me, Angel + Turquoise = My Mother."

"A reminder of how up close and personal they are."

Aspiration

Colour: deep purple

Definition: A hope or ambition of achieving something. The action of pronouncing a sound with an exhalation of breath.

Origin: Late Middle English: from French aspirer or Latin aspirare, from ad- 'to' + spirare 'breathe'.

Prompts for you:

What is your first response to the word?

To the colour?

What else is there?

And, what else is there?

What are your experiences of Aspiration?

How would you define what Aspiration means to you?

What changes when you connect with your breath and deepen into your intuition?

Experiences:

"I aspire to be more connected to spirit, the universe and all the beauty in this world. I also aspire to help every living creature possible including myself."

"The colour purple always brings a spiritual meaning to me which correlates to reaching my highest aspirations."

"A reminder to breathe, to reach, to let things flow."

"Aspiration - first thought was breath. Breathe, pause. Wisdom is always in the pause."

"I actually looked up this work in the dictionary. My first thought was to breathe. But it is also a strong desire or ambition. So what aspiration do I have that is so strong in me that it is as important as breathing?"

"Allow myself to dream big reach for those goals and, yes, listen to your inspiration."

Authenticity

Colour: deep pink

Definition: The quality of being authentic. Of undisputed origin and not a copy; genuine.

Prompts for you:

What is your first response to the word?

To the colour?

What else is there?

And, what else is there?

What are your experiences of Authenticity?

How would you define what Authenticity means to you?

When you feel you are not being Authentic? And how do you know? How can you bring more Authenticity into your life?

Experiences:

"Being true to myself and others and being open and honest to myself and others. Pink: a colour of love, universal truth and love."

"Allowing myself to be authentic even if it does not fit the expectations of others. Pink - sending love to myself."

"Being true to myself."

"Being real and open about how I am feeling."

"Being true to myself, what a great reminder – and showing myself, more open."

"What I strive for every day."

Beauty

Colour: mid blue

Definition: A combination of qualities, such as ape, colour, or form, that pleases the aesthetic senses, especially the sight."

Prompts for you:

What is your first response to the word?

To the colour?

What else is there?

And, what else is there?

What are your experiences of Beauty?

How would you define what Beauty means to you?

Where do you see the beauty in yourself?

Experiences:

"Beauty is all around us, always there regardless of whether we take note or otherwise - but when we take the time to notice, it's everywhere and infiltrates into our being. Take time to notice."
"This has a soothing, supportive feeling."

"See my own beauty."

"I must say that I am enjoying the serendipitous connections these cards are bringing out. Today I am dreed in soft blue and white including a blue topaz ring in various shades which is not a usual colour for me to wear. This is also the time of year (late summer) when I begin to notice a faded blue in the sky. It makes me thing of nostalgia as we wind down, at least in here, the summer season and yes there is amazing beauty in that."

Beginnings

Colour: dark green

Definition: The point in time or space at which something begins (for 'beginning')

Prompts for you:

What is your first response to the word?

To the colour?

What else is there?

And, what else is there?

What are your experiences of Beginnings?

How would you define what Beginnings means to you?

Does the thought of Beginnings excite you? Or scare you?

Experiences:

"Could be beginning of a new chapter.... going to view a flat."

"A fresh start, wipe the slate clean and start again. A new chapter in my life. Green represents growth."

"School starts here, so this is perfect. My husband's new schedule starts too......lol. All of this means I get a new beginning, a fresh start. September always feels that way for me. The green feels rooted and earthy."

"Perfection."

"Each day is a new beginning."

"This is a good one. September is my month. It is the start of my solar year and this year we Virgos are supposed to be starting a new cycle."

Being

Colour: purple

Definition: Existence: "The nature or essence of a person"

Prompts for you:

What is your first response to the word?

To the colour?

What else is there?

And, what else is there?

What are your experiences of Being?

How would you define what Being means to you?

Experiences:

"Beautiful. I always get the message: Just BE. Being means just be, being me, coming alive. Thank you."

"Just BE. You are perfect just as you are, YOU are enough."

"What perfect synchronicity. A reminder came to me earlier today to return to a surrendered state of being when taking action."

"I SO resonate with Being. That's how I let my world flow and everything unfolds perfectly and divinely. Colour purple is so regal. I feel like the queen of my universe observing the gift of life."

Belief

Colour: dark blue

Definition: Something one accepts as true or real;
a firmly held opinion.

Prompts for you:

What is your first response to the word?

To the colour?

What else is there?

And, what else is there?

What are your experiences of Belief?

How would you define what Belief means to you?

Experiences:

"Blue is solidity, believing in yourself and your dreams first and following the intuitive path."

"Belief in myself and the decisions I am making, and that blue feels deeply calm and reassuring."

"Belief there is support around me. That blue is calming, like a hug of support."

"Self-belief is my first thought. Nothing else to add today. "

"It seems these cards are hitting the mark! I just signed up for a course that I was waffling on. Even wrote about it. I had to look at my beliefs of myself to break the negative talk circling around in my head to give myself permission to spend the money."

"Belief that life is good and knowing it always has and always will support me."

Blossoming

Colour: bright pink

Definition: Mature or develop in a promising or healthy way.

Prompts for you:

What is your first response to the word?

To the colour?

What else is there?

And, what else is there?

What are your experiences of Blossoming?

How would you define what Blossoming means to you?

Experiences:

"Blossoming into the fullest version of myself and my work - the colour; bright and vibrant which is actually how I am feeling today - particularly poignant as I have lilies, roses, sunflowers and a mixed lily bouquet - all bought for me this week - wonderful!"

"It brings to mind projects coming to fruition."

"My first impression is of a sweet blush - excitement & tenderness & anticipation."

Caring

Colour: dark green

Definition: Displaying kindness and concern for others.

Prompts for you:

What is your first response to the word?

To the colour?

What else is there?

And, what else is there?

What are your experiences of Caring?

How would you define what Caring means to you?

Experiences:

"Caring... a reminder to care for oneself, to nurture one's spirit, one's body, one's soul."

"Caring for myself before ring for others. Today, because I can, this means going back to bed for an hour."

"Reminds me to take care of myself as well as others! I think of action when I think of caring. It is one thing to care and quite another to show it."

Celebration

Colour: red

Definition: The action of celebrating an important day or event.

Prompts for you:

What is your first response to the word?

To the colour?

What else is there?

And, what else is there?

What are your experiences of Celebration?

How would you define what Celebration means to you?

Experiences:

"I am celebrating being alive in this spectacular time on Earth. Loving my life more by the day."

"Okay you had me stumped at first. This isn't a word I hear very often or give much thought to. Today I am celebrating me. I never say that, but it feels right today."

"Awesome, yes celebrate YOU and make it a habit."

"I love the vibrant colour that fits the word celebration very well. I will celebrate this day!"

"Celebrating another wonderful, awesome day!! The colour red is such a vibrant colour, goes very well with the word celebration! My morning journaling was done with a red pen!!"

"Celebrating my life, how far I have gone, celebrating my freedom, my peaceful nature and feeling grateful, also my birthday is coming up soon, so I am already in pre-celebration mood."

"I spotted this as I am reflecting this morning on the almost completion of our Homestart summer programme - it has been such a success and I am definitely in a joyous and celebratory mood - the colour is vibrant and uplifting."

Cherish

Colour: purple

Definition: Protect and care for (someone) lovingly. Hold (something) dear.

Prompts for you:

What is your first response to the word?

To the colour?

What else is there?

And, what else is there?

What are your experiences of Cherish?

How would you define what Cherish means to you?

Experiences:

"Cherish and embrace the beauty of the natural world I couldn't find immediate responses to some of this week's words - but when I read this, I somehow felt wrapped in a hug."

"Hold dear to my heart (my loved ones)."

"Cherish every moment of every day."

"Cherish myself."

"Cherish to me is to look after in the best way possible, and to hold space in my heart. Deep purple is a perfect colour for that for me, not only does it have regal links, but I love the colour."

"Cherish the good times, let go of the bad ones."

Choices

Colour: dark blue

Definition: A range of possibilities from which one or more may be chosen.

Prompts for you:

What is your first response to the word?

To the colour?

What else is there?

And, what else is there?

What are your experiences of Choices?

How would you define what Choices means to you?

Experiences:

"Just a quick reflection on a choice I made last night... went along to Miracles cafe, where Nick Williams was speaking. Had a great evening, met some lovely folk.... yep, good choice."

"Confirms my thoughts that life-changing choices lay ahead – all part of life's rich tapestry."

"It is quite a neutral word in that you can make good or bad choices."

"Today I am making choices around what website subscription to keep and which to unsubscribe to. I find that, for now at any rate, I waste way too much time reading than actually doing. So one of my life choices is to focus more on the doing."

Clarity

Colour: orange

Definition: The quality of being coherent and intelligible;
The quality of being easy to see or hear; sharpness of
image or sound; The quality of being certain or definite;
The quality of transparency or purity.

Origin: Middle English (in the sense 'glory, divine
splendour'): from Latin claritas, from clarus 'clear'. The
current sense dates from the early 17th century.

Prompts for you:

What is your first response to the word?

To the colour?

What else is there?

And, what else is there?

What are your experiences of Clarity?

How would you define what Clarity means to you?

Experiences:

"I am always seeking clarity. Bright orange signifies energy for me. Energy and clarity means movement, hopefully more movement and clarity toward my purpose and vision."

"Sitting alone in a quiet house. This is the perfect word for me. The orange implies passion and action. Getting clear about what I am passionate about."

"Seems to be the word of the day for me."

"I have no time to write now, so will sit with the word as I go about my day and see what emerges – with the intention that it will bring illumination."

"Deep inside I know there is absolute clarity, like a steady, bright flame. Between where I feel I am just now and there, it feels…. Foggy, obscured a little."

"The colour orange for me, today, brings a balance from the mixture of red for vibrant emotion and action, and yellow for clarity and order. Orange feels balancing and enfolding, encouraging me to follow my intuition."

Communication

Colour: mid blue/dark turquoise

Definition: The imparting or exchanging of information by speaking, writing, or using some other medium.

Prompts for you:

What is your first response to the word?

To the colour?

What else is there?

And, what else is there?

What are your experiences of Communication?

How would you define what Communication means to you?

Experiences:

"Soft colour - reminder to speak soft words."

"The colour is a reminder to me to just let communication happen rather than forcing it. Learning to listen is part of communication. This month I began working with the daily card as part of my morning writing, one way of learning to listen."

"Good choice today as I start planning on how to bring more attention to my blog."

"Remembering to listen to my body is a part of communication I used to neglect, and I can very easily slip back into doing that, especially when very busy."

"Looking forward to a delicious morning of communication of the most direct kind, in person."

"For today, I will focus on communicating with those close around me and simply do the best I can. "

Courage

Colour: dark blue

Definition: The ability to do something that frightens one; bravery; Strength in the face of pain or grief.

Origin: Middle English (denoting the heart, as the seat of feelings): from Old French corage, from Latin cor 'heart'.

Prompts for you:

What is your first response to the word?

To the colour?

What else is there?

And, what else is there?

What are your experiences of Courage?

How would you define what Courage means to you?

Experiences:

"How appropriate. First day back at the day job today, and I need answers."

"My horoscopes for today say that with the new moon today, I am ending one chapter and beginning another now. This excites me and I am eager to get going. Courage is an appropriate word for me today."

"For me, the combination of word and colour strikes me. The feeling of courage being grounded in a strong, solid, reliable sort of colour. That seems to make it easier to imagine myself being 'courageous'."

Daring

Colour: bright 'apple' green

Definition: Adventurous courage:

Prompts for you:

What is your first response to the word?

To the colour?

What else is there?

And, what else is there?

What are your experiences of Daring?

How would you define what Daring means to you?

Experiences:

"The green is very light and uplifting."

"Daring .... feeling low key today, actually, which is rare these days - at a music festival this afternoon so, between now and then I'm planning to change my state from low to high key."

"A juxtaposition I know, but day to day, especially work wise, I'm DARING myself to 'flow' more rather than idea/quick response/action - possibly the reverse to many?!"

Emerging

Colour: brick red, the colour of red sandstone or desert soil.

Definition: Move out of or away from something and become visible; Become apparent or prominent.

Origin: Late 16th century (in the sense 'become known, come to light'): from Latin emergere, frome- (variant of ex-) 'out, forth' + mergere 'to dip'.

Prompts for you:

What is your first response to the word?

To the colour?

What else is there?

And, what else is there?

What are your experiences of Emerging?

How would you define what Emerging means to you?

Experiences:

"Red to me is two things, grounding and the reminder to ground but also it signifies an emergency, stop to see what emerges if you do stop and give yourself time to think, feel and emerge. Red is danger... warning us to stop."

"Emerging - coming out, stepping into your power. And the colour, a rich red, which immediately reminded me of our root chakra, which then made me think, we must be firmly rooted to fully emerge."

"The word of the day blends well with the topic of the blog I just posted. A personal topic for me but emerging gives me the feeling of anticipation."

Evolving

Colour: dark green.

Definition: Develop gradually.

Origin: Early 17th century (in the general sense 'make more complex, develop'): from Latin evolvere, from e- (variant of ex-) 'out of' + volvere 'to roll'.

Prompts for you:

What is your first response to the word?

To the colour?

What else is there?

And, what else is there?

What are your experiences of Evolving?

How would you define what Evolving means to you?

Experiences:

"Evolving to me and the green means change, growth and we're all doing that I'm our own way every day."

"For me the green feels very rooted and grounding and reminds me our evolving stems from our connection to ourselves and everything around us. This card feels like a hug today."

"Evolving and stepping up into my true self."

"Evolving from the bud to the flower. The green is welcoming, calming."

"I saw this as 'Evergreen' at first glance...and I like that!"

"Grounding, and growing. "

"Evolving? Not quite yet. But soon."

"Dark green speaks to me of earth and plants... evolving out of nature."

"I often see other words / transpose letters / etc. in everyday signs & written words....in 'Evolving' I first saw 'loving' and then 'Everything'...paired with that lovely rich green colour, this card speaks to me of growth - collective...One Love."

Faith

Colour: deep purple

Definition: Complete trust or confidence in someone or something.

Prompts for you:

What is your first response to the word?

To the colour?

What else is there?

And, what else is there?

What are your experiences of Faith?

How would you define what Faith means to you?

How does it feel when you lose Faith?

Can you still go on?

Experiences:

"Faith in oneself. Faith in your connection to the higher spirit. Faith in mankind. Pretty much how I roll."

"This is a reminder to me to 'let it be'. I put the work in, I need to have faith that it will come to fruition."

"A lot has been moving and shifting. Some of this has been testing my faith in myself and my work. Some reaffirming that faith. I need to go back and review and reflect."

"The colour strikes me first today, deep and rich. A combination of peaceful reflective blue and active red. A balance. Turning then to the word. Today, for me, faith has to be a balance, between action and acceptance."

.

Flexibility

Colour: soft purple/lavender

Definition: The quality of bending easily without breaking; Willingness to change or compromise.

Prompts for you:

What is your first response to the word?

To the colour?

What else is there?

And, what else is there?

What are your experiences of Flexibility?

How would you define what Flexibility means to you?

Experiences:

"As always divine timing. This word came up from my physicality and old habits at my massage therapy yesterday."

"I'm loving how flexible my body is becoming."

"Maybe the key today is simply, be flexible, see what the day brings, relax, go with the flow. The purple feels soft and strong at the same time, allowing me that choice."

"Like my body, sometimes it feels as if my mind, my brain itself, is stiff and inflexible. What can I do to loosen that up? Relax, meditate, read?"

"A good word for today, lots going on, with the need to be flexible – about arrangements, plans, ideas."

Forgiveness

Colour: orange

Definition: The action or process of forgiving or being forgiven.

Prompts for you:

What is your first response to the word?

To the colour?

What else is there?

And, what else is there?

What are your experiences of Forgiveness?

How would you define what Forgiveness means to you?

Experiences:

"Forgiveness... something I come back to quite regularly. Today it is a reminder to forgive me, to be kind to me, to not beat myself up over things done / not done.... breathing kindness and that helps me to be for giving... giving out, once I have gifted forgiveness to me...."

"Self-forgiveness is something I have to work at. The orange reminds me it is an action, not merely a word. Sitting with this today."

"Straight away my reaction was forgive yourself."

"My husband and I were talking about forgiveness this morning. Forgiving people even if they don't ask for it because it releases us. Forgiving ourselves for not meeting the expectations we have of ourselves, that often come from our family or parents or significant others, even when we don't realize we have the expectations. How perfect that this is today's card!"

"No react to this word for me. I readily forgive because I purposely choose to not let the energy of strife and anger weigh me down. Let that ** go!!"

Fun

Colour: bright pink

Definition: Enjoyment, amusement, or light-hearted pleasure.

Prompts for you:

What is your first response to the word?

To the colour?

What else is there?

And, what else is there?

What are your experiences of Fun?

How would you define what Fun means to you?

Is there a part of you that feels you don't deserve to have Fun?

How would it feel to simply allow Fun to be present?

Experiences:

"A calming colour exuding vibrant warmth to spice up the senses!"

"Fun....something I've had missing in my life lately but I feel the need for now. The red colour screams to me that fun is important to me now. Looking to find fun today Mary...thanks for sharing this card!"

"I started smiling and had the urge to giggle."

"It's my birthday today so I hope I have some fun!"

Generosity

Colour: deep yellow/light orange

Definition: The quality of being kind and generous; The quality or fact of being plentiful or large.

Prompts for you:

What is your first response to the word?

To the colour?

What else is there?

And, what else is there?

What are your experiences of Generosity?

How would you define what Generosity means to you?

Experiences:

"Do one kind act of generosity today. I will."

"Today, the colour reminds me of gold ingots, and thus money. I am not usually giving of my money, but I do donate to charity shops (I did the other day to rid myself of some clutter)."

"Generosity and the colour, solar plexus and Sacral chakra, when you give to others it not only makes them feel good it makes you feel good too, giving you both a glow of happiness more generosity and less selfish greed is needed in this world, then everyone will glow and shine their light. It's a colour of sunshine and happiness reminding us to be free, to enjoy the sunshine, be in nature and be happy. "

"Despite a full schedule myself I am cooking for everyone for when they get back tired, hungry and bedraggled - and doing it with love and a generous heart, as I have done in recent years .....poignant because it shows how far I've come - as a non-sailor, married to a sailor for over thirty years I have, in years gone by felt le than generous and full on resentment at times - 'GOLDEN' times."

"Being generous to myself, allowing myself to just be."

Gratitude

Colour: deep purple.

Definition: The quality of being thankful; readiness to show appreciation for and to return kindness.

Prompts for you:

What is your first response to the word?

To the colour?

What else is there?

And, what else is there?

What are your experiences of Gratitude?

How would you define what Gratitude means to you?

Experiences:

"It's funny how the universe hands you little lessons. I was awake early stressing about all the annoying things that have gone wrong with my renovations and then I see this word. I am humbled."

"Reminding to be thankful for what I have right now, to not worry on too far ahead, colour deeply calming and invokes sense of trust."

"Today I am overwhelmed with gratitude for all the support I am receiving from all around me."

Honesty

Colour: orange.

Definition: The quality of being honest: A European plant with purple or white flowers and round, flat, translucent seed pods which are used for indoor flower arrangements.

Origin: Middle English, from Old French honeste, from Latin honestas, from honestus. The original sense was 'honour, respectability', later 'decorum, virtue, chastity'. The plant is so named from its seed pods, translucency symbolizing lack of deceit.

Prompts for you:

What is your first response to the word?

To the colour?

What else is there?

And, what else is there?

What are your experiences of Honesty?
How would you define what Honesty means to you?

Experiences:

"What is it about this that makes people do the opposite?"

"That's my colour: beautiful orange exuding rays of warmth and honesty."

"Today this is about being honest to myself. Honest about how I am feeling, about ow things are going, about when I am tired and need to rest. If I am not able to be honest with myself, how can I do that with others?"

Hope

Colour: deep pink.

Definition: A feeling of expectation and desire for a particular thing to happen; Grounds for believing that something good may happen.

Prompts for you:

What is your first response to the word?

To the colour?

What else is there?

And, what else is there?

What are your experiences of Hope?
How would you define what Hope means to you?

Experiences:

"I need some hope."

"Deep pink ....thoughtful optimism - there is always hope but sometimes we need to dig deep for it ...."

"For myself today, I hope I can remember how to feed and change a month old baby - off to give my niece some respite an hour west along the coast."

"There is always hope. I think people sometimes confuse hope with wanting a specific outcome, but to me hope is one of the cornerstones of faith in the universe."

"Well I got up extra early and headed off to the construction store with my brother (my contractor) in high hopes of getting all the supplies I need for the renovation job. I had hope, I felt positive, I felt in control. Was that too much to hope for? Perhaps."

"There is always hope."

Joy

Colour: deep pink.

Definition: A feeling of great pleasure and happiness.

Origin: Middle English from Old French joie, based on Latin gaudium, from gaudere 'rejoice'.

Prompts for you:

What is your first response to the word?

To the colour?

What else is there?

And, what else is there?

What are your experiences of Joy?

How would you define what Joy means to you?

Do you remember that childlike feeling of skipping for joy for no particular reason? Can you bring that feeling into your life today?

Experiences:

"Hahahahaha..... nice one.... I am about to start packing up / sorting out stuff for my upcoming move out of London..... I am now wondering what I can do to make this a more joyful experience..."

"On a dark morning with the rain pouring down outside, this card made me smile. A reminder for me to find the joy in every moment."

"I could write a long 'joy list' – not from the thought that I should be happy, but rather that I choose to express my joy within, that childlike excitement at everything."

"This feeling of joy is so good, why would I choose not to feel it?"

Kindness

Colour: orange.

Definition: The quality of being friendly, generous, and considerate.

Prompts for you:

What is your first response to the word?

To the colour?

What else is there?

And, what else is there?

What are your experiences of Kindness?

How would you define what Kindness means to you?

Experiences:

"The phrase 'random acts of kindness' comes into my mind."

"The warm orange colour is cosy and comforting, bringing some brightness on a dark morning."

"Kindness softens and relaxes; soothes and calms; helps release tension and stress. It may be a smile, a word, a touch, being polite on the roads in traffic. Kindness has a ripple effect spreading out and out and passing on to many others."

Laughter

Colour: brick red, earthy red.

Definition: The action or sound of laughing.

Prompts for you:

What is your first response to the word?

To the colour?

What else is there?

And, what else is there?

What are your experiences of Laughter?

How would you define what Laughter means to you?

Experiences:

"I need more laughter in my life."

"Laughter is the medicine of the inner child. I need to hang out with mine more often."

"Belly laughs with a friend, giggles and snorts - I love laughing."

"This word brought a wee smile to my face. I've been a bit sad this week missing my dad whose birthday is coming up. Laughter reminded me of something mom (who has Alzheimer's) said yesterday about laughter and medicine. I think she was trying to remember the old adage laughter is the best medicine."

Learning

Colour: soft purple/lavender.

Definition: The acquisition of knowledge or skills through study, experience, or being taught.

Prompts for you:

What is your first response to the word?

To the colour?

What else is there?

And, what else is there?

What are your experiences of Learning?

How would you define what Learning means to you?

Experiences:

"I love the colour and I always feel that I am learning something."

"I am a true believer in the power of learning. We n always change our worldly circumstances if we are open and willing to learn."

"Never stop learning - when you do, you die. Life is all about moving forward, learning and transforming - it's my favourite colour and learning new stuff is my favourite thing! There's so much to know out there and the more you learn the more you realise there's so much more to learn."

Light

Colour: deep yellow/light orange.

Definition: The natural agent that stimulates sight and makes things visible. (Author's note: so many different uses of this word, and thus definitions).

Prompts for you:

What is your first response to the word?

To the colour?

What else is there?

And, what else is there?

What are your experiences of Light?

How would you define what Light means to you?

Experiences:

"To me in this moment, this card reminds me of a fire burning... lighting up a dark night sky..... I know I am waiting for the dawn.. when the sun will replace the fire and drench everything in light, making it easy to see the things that I am missing at the moment."

"I love this card, it instantly made me smile and think Thank God. I had a bit of a rough night with personal stuff and this card brings a beautiful ray of sunshine into my heart. Thank you Mary it was very much needed."

"Reminding us all that the sunshine, God's ray of bright guiding light is always there, even if it's hidden by cloud, it IS there, you are NEVER alone."

"The colour reminds me of the warmth of the sun, which I have missed recently. The word Light - I would like to feel lighter - more buoyant than I feel today."

"Ignite the light within."

"I am sitting out on my deck in the morning light."

Love

Colour: deep pink.

Definition: A strong feeling of affection; A great interest and pleasure in something.

Prompts for you:

What is your first response to the word?

To the colour?

What else is there?

And, what else is there?

What are your experiences of Love?

How would you define what Love means to you?

Experiences:

"Nothing needs to be said on this one."

"My first response is reminding myself of self-love."

Note: I feel I need to comment here: this card is one that many of us feel unable to write about. It seems to be more of a feeling than anything else.

So, here is a quote attributed to Oscar Wilde:

"Keep love in your heart. A life without it is like a sunless garden when the flowers are dead."

Meditation

Colour: dark green

Definition: The action or practice of meditating: (to focus one's mind for a period of time, in silence or with the aid of chanting, for religious or spiritual purposes or as a method of relaxation)

Prompts for you:

What is your first response to the word?

To the colour?

What else is there?

And, what else is there?

What are your experiences of Meditation?

How would you define what Meditation means to you?

Experiences:

"Some deep thinking needed today. And, given the colour, maybe in nature."

"A great reminder to really get back into my daily meditation practice."

"This prompts me to think about focus and depth. And, those are the only words I have just now."

"Meditate came to mind this morning. Negotiating a balance between inner and outer worlds, between the heart and the mind, between what you feel and what you know. The dark green is the path to balance."

"This has been nudging me gently all week. Make space. Quiet the noise. Be present."

"Peacefulness, the smell of green, pine, memories of childhood vacations at a lake, damp earth smell, soft forest floor."

Opportunity

Colour: deep pink

Definition: A time or set of circumstances that makes it possible to do something.

Prompts for you:

What is your first response to the word?

To the colour?

What else is there?

And, what else is there?

What are your experiences of Opportunity?

How would you define what Opportunity means to you?

Experiences:

"The opportunity to transform the world today."

"The opportunity to transform my life and help others in the process."

"The opportunity to choose what I want to feel in every moment....joy happiness, peace, well-being."

"Each new moment brings the gift of new opportunities."

"The opportunity to cultivate a greater heart-centred experience of Life!"

"The opportunity to simply have a great day."

"It makes me smile, and reminds me that opportunities are there for the taking."

"The word and the colour excite me!"

Patience

Colour: dark green

Definition: The capacity to accept or tolerate delay, problems, or suffering without becoming annoyed or anxious.

Origin: Middle English: from Old French, from Latin patientia, from patient- 'suffering', from the verb pati.

Prompts for you:

What is your first response to the word?

To the colour?

What else is there?

And, what else is there?

What are your experiences of Patience?

How would you define what Patience means to you?

Experiences:

Feeling this sense of urgency to get it all done now. I am guessing this is how a farmer feels at this time of year. A good reminder to be patient with myself. And the Universe."

"Reminding myself to have patience with others' rhythms as I visit family."

"Understanding some things just take longer – like building your website."

Peace

Colour: soft mid blue.

Definition: Freedom from disturbance; tranquillity.

Prompts for you:

What is your first response to the word?

To the colour?

What else is there?

And, what else is there?

What are your experiences of Peace?

How would you define what Peace means to you?

Experiences:

"A reminder that Peace is always there within, always accessible if I n only detach a little from the sometimes frantic everyday world. Detach and reconnect with the quiet within, that still quiet place of refuge."

"A nice way to see the new week ahead. Be at peace with what you cannot change, but positive with what you can."

"Peace - feeling very organised (rare for Sagittarius me!) and this week is to be complete downtime - thinking, planning, being and lots of FUN."

"Peace ... inner peace, calm and being blue, communicate in a peaceful, calm manner."

"Blue is a peaceful colour for me."

"Oh yes please, lots and lots of peace."

Power

Colour: purple.

Definition: The ability or capacity to do something or act in a particular way. (Author's note: many definitions of this word.)

Origin: Middle English from Anglo-Norman French poeir, from an alteration of Latin posse 'be able'.

Prompts for you:

What is your first response to the word?

To the colour?

What else is there?

And, what else is there?

What are your experiences of Power?

How would you define what Power means to you?

Experiences:

"A feeling of being in control without acting on impulse."

"To know that I have the ability to meet any situation that may arise."

"For this moment - my hands have new power to soothe and heal. The colour isn't speaking to me yet today."

"We have a power to do what we wish to. The colour has regal connections."

"Purple to me gives me the sign through my 3rd eye that spirit are around, ready to work and assist.

"Power of spirit, your own inner power, reminding us we can achieve anything if we tap into our inner strength and ask for spirits assistance. Girl power!!"

"I love purple, my favourite colour."

"For me the colour purple will always be associated with the divine so purple power is my connection to the divine which I know, for me, is the ultimate power."

"My favourite colour, too. Personal power, divination, listening."

Purpose

Colour: purple.

Definition: The reason for which something is done or created or for which something exists; A person's sense of resolve or determination.

Prompts for you:

What is your first response to the word?

To the colour?

What else is there?

And, what else is there?

What are your experiences of Purpose?

How would you define what Purpose means to you?

Experiences:

"Every day has a purpose, it's up to each individual to decide what that purpose is. There is so much to choose from in this busy world."

"Doing the day 'on purpose '"

"My first thought is that this is a strong work. Combined with a soft yet powerful colour. A quiet determined strength. And that is something I would like to bring into my day."

Relaxation

Colour: mid blue

Definition: The state of being free from tension and anxiety.

Prompts for you:

What is your first response to the word?

To the colour?

What else is there?

And, what else is there?

What are your experiences of Relaxation?

How would you define what Relaxation means to you?

Experiences:

"It's something I need more of!"

"Perfect. Yoga this morning that stretched out the stuck bits. A walk by the river with my daughter. A hot cup of tea on an unexpectedly cooler morning."

"It's something I need more of and the colour blue to me is communication, so maybe we need to communicate and start delegating some jobs and tasks to others so we n relax more."

"Relaxation for me means, doing what I love to do and allowing myself to do nothing let the Inspiration flow and take it as it comes."

"I decided to sit outside enjoy the feel of the summer breeze and catch up on my Facebook feed for 15 min instead of my usual Saturday morning routine."

"Taking breaths between busy moments all day, then a nap, and next, dinner and a movie with my three daughters - their suggestion – BFG!"

Self-love

Colour: soft purple/lavender.

Definition: Regard for one's own well-being and happiness.

Prompts for you:

What is your first response to the word?

To the colour?

What else is there?

And, what else is there?

What are your experiences of Self-love?

How would you define what Self-love means to you?

Experiences:

"Self-love is vital, they say if you don't love yourself then how can you expect others to love you, be kind to yourself, say nice things to yourself, give yourself praise. Never speak bad of yourself for it will upset and hurt your soul. Love yourself always and remember you are perfect in God's eyes."

"Love the colour- Energising and uplifting. I read the word today as loving who you are and what you do."

"With nerves kicking in for a big 48 hours at work, it says to me be proud of what you can do, love what you do and what you have and how your actions can help and support others."

"For me, today it means being soft and gentle with myself. It may also mean loving myself enough to get my accounts in order."

Serenity

Colour: mid blue.

Definition: The state of being calm, peaceful, and untroubled.

Origin: Late Middle English: from Old French serenite, from Latin serenitas, from serenus 'clear, fair'.

Prompts for you:

What is your first response to the word?

To the colour?

What else is there?

And, what else is there?

What are your experiences of Serenity?

How would you define what Serenity means to you?

Experiences:

"Peace and calm. "

"Mmm.. I am sinking into to it like a soft cloud."

"Feeling 'at peace' with where I am in life at the moment .... so grateful."

"Calm & cool."

"Adds a spirit of peace, an aura where one can reside in pure relaxation."

Support

Colour: deep pink.

Definition: Bear all or part of the weight of; hold up: Middle English (originally in the sense 'tolerate'): from Old French supporter, from Latin supportare, from sub- 'from below' + portare 'carry'.

Prompts for you:

What is your first response to the word?

To the colour?

What else is there?

And, what else is there?

What are your experiences of Support?

How would you define what Support means to you?

Experiences:

"Pink... loving heart and pink crystal angels.... have been calling on Universe for support in many ways lately. Also appreciation of the support given to me by friends."

"Asking for support, when needed."

"Lovely pink. Always the colour behind my eyes during meditation."

"A hard one for me but I also know that to move forward in life you need to ask and allow support."

"Receiving can be a challenge for many people. I like to remember it is part of a cycle. If you refuse support it's like telling the universe to stop bringing an abundance of good into your life."

"Decluttering is difficult. Without support!"

Surrender

Colour: dark green.

Definition: Give in to (a powerful emotion or influence).
Stop resisting to an enemy or opponent and submit to
their authority.

Prompts for you:

What is your first response to the word?

To the colour?

What else is there?

And, what else is there?

What are your experiences of Surrender?

How would you define what Surrender means to you?

Experiences:

"Perfect word for today. The colour signifies peace for me. Surrender to peace."

"Perfect card for me, I felt tired a bit worn out lately and today I just decided to just be and surrender - fab"

"It is a reminder that sometimes you just have to step back and trust in the universe."

"What will be will be. Would be nice to go with this a bit more!"

Synchronicity

Colour: deep pink.

Definition: The simultaneous occurrence of events which appear significantly related but have no discernible causal connection.

Prompts for you:

What is your first response to the word?

To the colour?

What else is there?

And, what else is there?

What are your experiences of Synchronicity?

How would you define what Synchronicity means to you?

Experiences:

"I love when I experience synchronicity. For me it is like being loved and supported by God."

"Great timing happens at random."

"Love this word! Firstly, the look of it on the page, and the way it rolls: syn-chron-icity... beautiful."

Understanding

Colour: turquoise/aqua blue.

Definition: The ability to understand something; comprehension; Sympathetic awareness or tolerance.

Prompts for you:

What is your first response to the word?

To the colour?

What else is there?

And, what else is there?

What are your experiences of Understanding?

How would you define what Understanding means to you?

Experiences:

"Understanding is what you perceive to be true, your understanding of any given thing, but always practice compassion with this understanding, with yourself and others."

"Turquoise is to me a combination of blue and green, throat and heart combined, so yet again speak your truth from your heart with love and compassion."

"Turquoise blue is one of my favourite colours. I feel at peace when I see it. Understanding each other's position can lead to peace."

Wisdom

Colour: turquoise/aqua blue.

Definition: The quality of having experience, knowledge, and good judgement; the quality of being wise.

Prompts for you:

What is your first response to the word?

To the colour?

What else is there?

And, what else is there?

What are your experiences of Wisdom?

How would you define what Wisdom means to you?

Experiences:

"First thoughts, something about wisdom I gained from my mother, and how much of that I am able to pass on to others every day- colour, gentle, soft."

"Feeling so sad today Too much loss and heaviness. Wisdom is what gets us through. Blue is soothing. Thank you."

"Ahhhh, my favourite topic. I love that it is green to connect to the heart chakra because true wisdom must come from the heart."

References and Resources

All definitions and notes on the origins of the words are from http://www.oxforddictionaries.com. (Accessed in summer 2016.)

As mentioned at the beginning of this book, you can buy your own pack of Dare to Blossom Rediscovery Cards direct from me via my website www.daretoblossom.co.uk

There you will also find links to my original artwork, my greetings cards of art and photography, and details of my coaching services. If you would like to experience how I work for yourself, please contact me there to book a complimentary consultation.

At the bottom of the 'Welcome' page you will find a link to sign up to the monthly newsletter to receive news and details of workshops and online programmes, along with a reflective article and links to other inspirational people I come across in my work.

I also have an active Facebook page, and a dedicated group where we discuss a card as starting point or a meditation for each day. Just search for 'Dare to Blossom Life Coaching'.

www.ingramcontent.com/pod-product-compliance
Lightning Source LLC
Chambersburg PA
CBHW070107070426
42448CB00038B/1839